Hunter's Blueprint

Winning Strategies for Navigating the Modern Employment Landscape

Copyright ©2023 Chalya Princess Miri-Gazhi
All rights reserved.
ISBN 978-1-913455-60-6
No part of this book shall be reproduced or transmitted in any form or by any means, electronic or mechanical, including photocopying, recording, or by any information retrieval system without prior written permission of the author and publisher.
Published by Scribblecity Publications United Kingdom.
Printed in Great Britain.
Although every precaution has been taken in the preparation of this book, the publisher and author assume no responsibility for errors or omissions. Neither is any liability assumed for damages resulting from the use of this information contained herein.

Dedication

The Lord God has given me the tongue of the learned,
that I should know how to speak a word in season to those
who are weary. (Isaiah 50:4)

This book is dedicated to those who are weary, employment-wise, and to the millions of hardworking job seekers, including those seeking a career change, who, though terrified of navigating the modern employment landscape, are determined to do something about it.

Acknowledgements

In writing this acknowledgement, I must thank my ever-faithful companion, guide, counsellor, mentor and friend, who has been with me every step of the way. In and out of season, to correct, caution, and encourage my small steps that led eventually to the completion of this book – thank You Holy Spirit! I love you very much and I am forever indebted to you. *Ndinci byet*.

I thank Bolaji Osime, my dearest friend and buddy, whose life is a shining example of what it means to be determined, focused, hardworking and relentless at going after one's professional goals and dreams. She is an embodiment of all the great traits and qualities of a 21st century tech-savvy entrepreneur that this book underscores but especially, a stellar example of an apostle in the marketplace. As a dogged reformer and nation builder, she inspires me no doubt, with her driven passion to see every child get quality and affordable education in Nigeria whilst striving for the spiritual transformation of hearts and minds in Nigeria. God bless you BJ.

My special thanks go to the Ruxton and Richmond House church members: Sheri Adegbenro who challenged me back on the recruitment path; Daniel Akapo, Rele Adesina and Dr Carlton Williams whose nurturing messages were the wings upon which I flew and the fires that thawed away my unresponsiveness, galvanizing me towards transforming (and terraforming) my small recruitment corner into an impactful space for touching lives.

I thank all members of my family for their constant love and prayers on my behest. A special thanks to my darling mom, Mrs Sally Alice Miner Nee Miri-Gazhi, Nannyi Winnifred Samuel, Kurcit Achemu, Zinkur Samuel Miri-Gazhi, Parya Miri-Gazhi and Yankat Faseluka. I extend my thanks to Kenneth Aku Achemu, Samuel Sabo Nimmyel and Rose Miri-Gazhi.

In a world of digital associations through various virtual platform groups, I thank these Whatsapp groups for being an enabling environment that foster spiritual development, professional advancement, cultural and emotional intelligence: the Nigerian Nation Builders Group (NNBG), Education Reforms Innovative Team (ERIT), Transformed Minds, Think on This Initiative (TOT), and Ngapak. I am particularly grateful to my spiritual big brother, Ayodele Adeboye for his ceaseless encouragement, prayers and relentless support for this book, and how he made time to always correct and spur me on whenever I was wearied. God, bless you lots bro Ayo!!!

Having these talented professionals endorse my work was humbling. I am grateful for all the endorsers of my book and their endorsements seen herein. I am also grateful to Nanna Yakubu, a fellow author, for giving me great pointers and support needed to navigate the publishing world.

I love that I have certain friends who have always supported my personal, spiritual and professional growth just because they believe in me and see great stuff in me that I didn't think I had, pushing me on in the kindest possible ways, to be better, stronger and greater. Special

thanks to my dear friend Debbie Braimoh, who has always been a true inspiration and helper in no small measure and in the kindest of ways; much thanks to Kassim Ahmed, Vince Osawe, Dr Ngozi Azodoh, Bolanle Onagoruwa, Rev. Solomon Kuje, Rose Ndong, and John Eziaghighala. I thank my cheering squad of friends: Nunu Obi, Sammy Omotese, Rinmicit Aboki, Seyive Boya and Sandra Barnabas.
I commend Annie Okpaleke for her selfless support and tireless encouragement for my book. Her kindness and generosity are immeasurable. Thank you, Annie.
My great gratitude goes to all the staff of Global International College (GIC), Philip Ademola and to my curious but quick learning assistant, Nneoma Precious Great.
Finally, thank you Barbara Ifezue and Scribblecity Publishing Team for your invaluable professional and enthusiastic support that went into shaping this book into what it has now become.

Endorsements

The Job Hunter's Blueprint is indeed a practical blueprint that is pragmatic, easy to understand and follow through for definite results. It is loaded with power nuggets that can accelerate your career progress, and if followed methodically, can land you on the path to the career of your dreams. It is practical, applicable and contains very vital information on how to navigate the entire course of your career, whether you are just starting out, or stuck in a rut.

-Soluchy Agu
Talent Specialist & Peformance Coach
www.soluchiconsult.com

This book is specially tailored to meet the demand of job seekers in the contemporary world where both private and public sectors are saturated. *The Job Hunter's Blueprint* has brought to the fore, the relevant skills job seekers are expected to possess to make them fit for today's intensely competitive job market. It is a good companion for young job seekers who are anxious about knowing how to find entry point into the labour market. The book is strongly recommended for all youth and particularly those who are expecting to find profitable accommodation in the labour market."

- *Professor Nanven Gambo,*
Vice-Chancellor, Karl Kumm University Vom, Jos South LGA,
Plateau State-Nigeria

In the book, *The Job Hunter's Blueprint*, Chalya Princess Miri-Gazhi has written an invaluable guide to navigating the complex job market in the 21st century. Computers and technology in general have re-defined the world of work and literally obliterated the 9-5 paradigm. With simple engaging prose, Miri-Gazhi walks the potential job hunter through a process that is sure to yield the right outcome. I heartily recommend this fine book to all readers."

- *Ikhide R. Ikheloa*
Literary and Social Critic

One of the *The Job Hunter's Blueprint's* standout features is its holistic approach to job hunting. It doesn't just focus on writing a standout CV or mastering the interview process; it guides the reader through each step of the journey. It begins with helping you assess your skills and defining your career goals, and continues through to the negotiation of your salary and how to excel in your new workplace.

Abolaji Osime
CEO Global International College & Global Reimagine Online Academy

Contents

Acknowledgements	v
Endorsements	ix
Foreword	xix

1. FIRST THINGS FIRST   23
- Assessing Your Skills and Defining Your Career Goals: Aligning your strengths with your dream job

2. PINPOINTING THE JOB   42
- Crafting a Winning Job Search Strategy: Maximizing your search efforts for optimal results

3. PUTTING YOURSELF OUT THERE   53
- Distinctive CVs, and Job Application Letters: Designing materials that capture attention

4. SELLING YOURSELF AT THE INTERVIEW   73
- Nailing the Job Interview: Mastering the art of selling yourself

5. PUTTING A PRICE TAG TO YOUR SKILLS   87
- Negotiating Salary and Benefits: Getting what you're worth

6. GIVING VALUE WHEN YOU GET ON BOARD   94
- Excelling in Your New Role at the Work Place: Strategies for long-term success

7. MOVING FORWARD ON YOUR CAREER PATH   103
- Navigating Career Transitions: Pivoting with purpose

Foreword

In a dynamic and interconnected global economy marked by increasingly uniform standards of competition and expectation, finding and keeping a job and a professional pathway to self-fulfilment is a daunting task. This is why Chalya Princess Miri-Gazhi's *The Job Hunter's Blueprint* is a timely and, forgive the tautology, invaluable blueprint for those trying to navigate the job market of 21st century global and national economies.

In one concise and easily readable volume, Miri-Gazhi, a professional recruiter with a vast international recruitment consulting repertoire, offers guidance that are both educational and practical. The inspirational and educational dimension of the book is its clear articulation of what a job seeker needs to understand and how they need to position themselves to be competitive.

Miri-Gazhi provides a robust expert definition of the foundational and ubiquitous job market concept of "skills," explaining the two overlapping categories of knowledge-based and applied skills. She then carefully and clearly lets the reader into why acquiring, updating, and clearly communicating one's repertoire of skills to potential employers are the gold standards of job hunting in our modern knowledge- and skill-driven economy.

The educational aspect of this book also tackles an intangible but highly consequential element in job hunting: self-presentation. This is an area in which many job applicants fall short, either short-selling themselves or over-doing the self-sell. Miri-Gazhi weighs in to explain the intricacies of first defining yourself, finding your core strengths, and then matching those strengths pragmatically to your professional aspirations.

As she convincingly demonstrates in the book, this art of finding one's strengths and pitching them in the right frame to register with potential employers is relevant to both fresh graduates seeking a foot in the career door and seasoned professionals trying to change jobs or career paths.

The practical aspect of the book is a veritable harvest of detailed, usable guides to the job search process.

It contains broad guidelines for preparing for and executing an effective job search strategy. It also addresses the nitty-gritties of how to apply and interview for job openings and, once the job is secured, maximize one's starting and continuing positions in the job. Miri-Gazhi's recruitment consultancy experience is on full display here as she outlines and explains the granular details and the how-to steps a job seeker must implement to succeed.

From preparing winning resumes and CVs to crafting supporting documents to acing different types of job interviews to negotiating an offer and thriving in a new job, The Job Hunter's Blueprint offers the reader a close and practical entry into the world of effective job hunting. It demonstrates in accessible prose the elements that stand a job candidate out from competitors and make the applicant memorable to employers.

All those applying for jobs and competitive professional opportunities as first-time job seekers or experienced professionals will benefit immensely from buying and reading this book. The book brims with professional insight and tested expert counsel, and it is my hope that it will correct many misunderstandings about the job market and transform the way many people navigate it.

~ Moses E Ochonu
Cornelius Vanderbilt Chair and Professor of African History, Vanderbilt University, Nashville, USA.

— 1 —

FIRST THINGS FIRST

Assess Your Skills and Define Your Career Goals: Align your strengths with your dream job

There are times we feel stuck in a rut, as if our career has stalled. All the indicators on the dashboard are blinking and we're not sure what exactly is wrong, how to fix things and get moving again. How on  earth do we recover power and momentum? Like you, I've been there before. The first step when we get to this junction, with respect to finding that dream job that will spring us out of the rut, is to assess skills and define career goals. Therefore, in this chapter, we will explore how to identify skills and discover true passions. First, though, let's talk about the meaning of a skill, types of skills, and their classifications.

Types of Skills

What is a skill? A skill is an activity you can carry out in a competent manner. It's as simple as that. There are many types of skills that can be classified under three main categories:

- **Professional or Knowledge-based Skills**
- **Transferable Skills**
- **Practical Skills**

Professional or Knowledge-Based Skills: are often called Technical Skills. These are skills you acquire through training, practice or experience. For example, you can obtain Computer Literacy Skills by practicing at home or at your workplace; using a computer over and over to the point that you become proficient at computer usage. Similarly, you may be adept at speaking French because you acquired training through a formal education. In other words, you attended lessons where you were taught professionally how to speak French, with access to a language laboratory equipped with audio gadgets.

You probably had practical sessions in the lab, and thereafter went on internships to France to perfect your French speaking and writing. You might also gain on-the-job experience of accounting apps, learning how to use Sage or Quick-Book as an accountant.

These are all specially acquired skills that your proficiency at them was made possible through practice, formal training or on-the-job training. In essence, when you have **Technical Skills**, you have sound knowledge of a subject and its application, or have abilities that you can deploy to perform a procedure. Examples of people with technical knowledge are myriad: these include professionals like heart surgeons, lawyers, data analysts, project managers, architects, administrators, facility or HR managers, etc. These abilities are usually expressed as nouns. People with professional skills have knowledge of industry-specific regulations, ethical standards, and best practices.

Transferable Skills: These are skills that you can apply in different industries. You can literally take these abilities from one job to another. Transferable skills are not specific to any particular job and are often more valuable in the long run, as they allow individuals to adapt to changing job markets and career paths.

Transferable skills can be further classified into two or more sub-categories, but let's stick to the two major classes which fall under Personal Skills and Cognitive Skills.

> **PERSONAL SKILLS:** These are skills that reflect your personality. They help you relate well with others and are behavioural in nature. They are sometimes called social skills. Examples include:
>
>   - ***Leadership Skills*** - Having the ability to inspire, guide, motivate, and direct others toward

achieving a shared objective.

- **Customer Service Skills** – Pertaining to someone with good customer service skills, and who has the ability to respond effectively to the needs of customers. Such a person knows how to provide excellent customer services and respond promptly to customers' inquiries.

- **Communication Skills**

- Having the ability to communicate effectively, through verbal or written means. You hear stuff like, "She is an effective communicator."

COGNITIVE SKILLS:

These are skills that require mental acuity. People with Cognitive Skills are perceptive and oftentimes detail-oriented. Their skill sets involve the use of logic and rational thinking. Individuals who possess cognitive skills pay proper attention to the key essentials of their job.

- **Problem Solving Skills** also fall into this category. People with problem-solving skills such as

Project Managers, are almost always prepared for eventualities and make provisions to address future outcomes long before a problem arises. They have the ability to identify, analyse, and solve problems using logic and critical thinking.
- *Analytical Skills* are part of this category, and involve having the ability to collate, analyse and interpret data in order to make informed decisions.

Practical Skills are skills that involve the use of hands-on techniques; the manipulation of tools or equipment. Examples of practical skills include sewing, dyeing of garments, carpentry, plumbing, woodwork, sculpting, and electrical work. Forms of artistry and professional athletics with a range of practitioners such as pro-footballers, basketball players, pianists, guitarist, designers, etc. are persons who can also be found in this subset.

It is important to note that some people may possess skill sets that fall into all the major categories above. You have medical doctors or engineers who are great golfers or exceptional pianists and who also possess analytical skills. I have seen architects who are excellent at woodwork. You may have just one skill or many skills, but you do NOT have NO skills. Experience has shown me that people tend to have at least one skill. I hear you ask, "…But what if I actually have no skills?" Interestingly, several people I have interviewed who think they have no skills usually have a skill, but that skill is simply not a good fit for the job they desire. Many do not even know that what they have is a skill.

Assessing Your Skills

Now that you know what a skill is and the different types of skills and their categories, it is time to assess the skills you have. This is important because assessing your skills is the first step in finding a job that is the right fit for you.

How do you do this? Start off by identifying your abilities. Make a comprehensive list of all that you can do competently. It does not matter if they seem useless to you. Write them down. This list could include technical, practical or transferable skills. Don't be afraid to include skills that you don't use in your current job, but you do have them.

Evaluate your Skills: Once you have a full list of your skills, evaluate them. First ask yourself some sincere questions. Be honest with your answers as what you are doing is akin to a mental scanning and SWOT analysis of your strengths and weaknesses. You are interviewing yourself, so you have nothing to be embarrassed about. Key questions to ask include: Which skills am I most proficient at? Which ones do I enjoy using the most? Which skills do I need to improve?

Identify your Strengths: Based on your evaluation, identify your strengths. These are the skills you're most proficient at and enjoy using the most. Your strengths are usually stuff you do effortlessly that people commend you for. They are things you do so well that people will come to you and ask for your help to get them done properly. Take into account the following to determine your strengths:

- **Your Training and Education:** What abilities and knowledge did you acquire while attending school or a training program?
- **Prior Employment:** In what areas of your previous employment did you excel? What are your proudest professional achievements?

- **Your Personality:** What qualities do you have that make you an asset to any company? Are you a good problem-solver, team player or communicator?

Knowing your strength is very important because you will need to highlight your strengths eventually in job search documents such as your resume, cover letter, and also on various professional platforms like your LinkedIn profile. This will position you to be noticed by the right potential employers and improve your chances of getting hired.

Look for reoccurring patterns: Look for functional patterns in your skills that seem to reoccur at every job you've held, whether paid or volunteer work. You may end up with more than one reoccurring pattern. For instance, you may find that you used your personal or soft skills or technical skills at every job you had. These are emerging transferable skills. Do you have a lot of technical skills? Are your personal skills your strongest asset? Understanding these patterns can help you identify the types of jobs that would be a good fit for you.

Seek Feedback:

Don't be afraid to ask others for feedback on your skills. Ask your colleagues, friends, and family members to provide insight on your strengths and on areas that need improvement.

Take Assessments: There are many online assessments that can help you identify your strengths and interests. These assessments can provide insight into career paths that align with your skills and passions.

> ***Story:*** Nanbyen had been working as an accountant for five years, but she wasn't happy on the job. She felt like she wasn't using her full potential and wanted to explore other career options. Nanbyen decided to make a list of her skills and discovered that she was good at problem-solving, paid attention to details, and

was competent at data analysis. She also realized that she enjoyed working with people and wanted a career that allowed her to interact with others more. With this newfound knowledge, Nanbyen started exploring other career options that aligned with her skills and passions. Today, she works as a data analyst at a management consultancy firm.

Defining Your Career Goals

Defining your career goals is the next step in finding your dream job. Here's how you can define your career goals:

Consider your Interests: Start by thinking about your interests. What do you enjoy doing? What kinds of activities or tasks do you find most fulfilling? Do you prefer outdoor work over indoor sit-in-the-office responsibilities?

Research Career Options: Once you've identified your interests, research career options that align with them. Look for jobs that require the skills you're good at and enjoy using. Use Google, use ChatGPT, check YouTube, and attend free master classes that teach about personal development. Also buy or download e-books on subject matters that interest you so you can read up on them. The world has become a global village. We live in an era of Information Technology. These days, all the information you need is available on several websites, blogs, in books and social media industry pages. Be thirsty like a dry sponge, ready to soak in all that you can from available faucets of knowledge.

Enrol to be Trained: Once you are sure of what career path you want to follow, and have determined what skills you have or do not have, you can enrol for an appropriate course toward getting some formal training on the path you want to pursue. Being trained in what you love doing makes you even better at it. Every industry has its standards, and training will equip you with best industry practices, while providing you proper certification that qualifies you to be well paid for what you do. Platforms like **Udemy, Khan Academy** and **Coursera** are online platforms that offer a wide variety of courses on various topics. They are equipped with different learning formats using lectures, videos, quizzes and other preparatory instructional materials to aid learning.

Two major aspects of training are **Acquiring New Skills** aka **Reskilling and Developing Skills** aka Upskilling. To reskill means you have to learn or acquire a new set of skills in an area where you have little or no knowledge or experience. Upskilling, however, is different. Upskilling adds to what you already have on the career path you want to pursue. It adds to your current skill sets.

- Acquiring and Developing Skills: *"Acquiring skills"* is the process of learning new skills or expanding knowledge and abilities. This can be done through a variety of methods, including formal education, online learning, or simply learning on the job. *"Developing skills"* refers to the process of honing and refining the skills that one already has and going higher with your proficiency level. This can be done through practice, experience, and feedback from others.

It pays to acquire new skills. By doing so, you become more marketable. Moreover, new skills improve your chances of getting promotions at the office. The reality is that the work place is becoming increasingly competitive. Having several skills puts you ahead of your colleagues and peer groups. It has the potential to elevate you into more prestigious positions with better perks. New skills expand your horizon and helps you stay relevant in your field, preventing you from becoming obsolete. Learning how to use new apps and software, learning how to deploy new digital productivity tools, learning a new language, or enrolling in culinary training to learn better cooking methods etc., all serve to make you more prepared for the future of the industry you work for or want to be part of. Beyond this, learning new skills can be stimulating and fun. It engages your intellectual capability, exercising your brain and stimulating new neural pathways. This helps to improve your cognitive abilities and boost mental powers. Research has shown that learning fresh skills improves memory, the ability to solve problems, and generally, helps us think more creatively.

On the other hand, **developing our skills** will help us become more effective and efficient at what we do. When we develop our skills, we are building on what we already have. We are refining our current abilities in order to become exceptional at what we do. Consider the situation of a worker in the Tech sector as an example. Technology is advancing quickly in this field. Look at how cable phones changed into analogue cell phones and later, smart phones. Mighty computers have morphed into desktops and laptops and now

IPads over time. We are seeing as well, the development of Artificial Intelligence, (AI) and Virtual Reality (VR). Workers in the technology industry must keep up with the most recent developments in their sector in order to stay relevant and competitive. Employees in the Tech industry might need to become proficient in cutting-edge technologies like AI or VR or master new coding languages. It would be challenging for computer workers to continue to contribute to their workplace without this continual professional development.

A chef who develops her skills, prepares better dishes in less time. A writer who develops her skills, writes better and ends up speaking better. A teacher who develops her skills teaches better and learns cutting edge pedagogical methods for delivering her lessons so that her students can easily understand. Developing your skills sets you well on your way to becoming proficient and ultimately, an expert in your chosen field.

As earlier mentioned, Udemy and Coursera are good examples of online learning platforms. Some courses are freely provided while other courses are provided for a fee depending on the course load. In addition, another great platform is Khan Academy which is an educational organization that is a great resource for anyone wanting to build their skills and knowledge. It offers free online courses, with a focus on skills that are in demand in the workplace like data analysis, coding, design, etc - an absolutely great online resource for learning. There are also other great platforms for lifelong learning and professional development: Semicolon Africa, Code Plateau and Cactus Tech are some of the many IT platforms that offer basic ICT training for those who want to pursue a career in programming, software applications and other related programs in Information Technology.

They offer instructor-led tech training courses like Tech Beginner Program, IT Support, Web Development (front end and back end), Tech Career Coaching and finding your niche in tech generally, including how to search and apply for tech roles. Another good example of sites where you can develop your skills is the website platform called SkilledUp Life. (www.skilledup.life) SkilledUp does a good job of linking Tech start-ups with qualified volunteers looking to gain valuable experience and skills. It offers opportunities for both companies and volunteers. Volunteers get to work on real life projects with companies purely for the purpose of gaining experience and improving abilities. Participants are not eligible to receive cash compensation or other taxable benefits, and companies are not permitted to make guarantees or offer remuneration to volunteers, so the talent is entirely free.

> **Story:** Nina studied Zoology at the University. Three years after her mandatory NYSC (National Youth Service Corp) year, she was still unable to get a well-paid job, so she settled for doing less satisfying jobs like working as a Receptionist, a Nanny or a Front Desk Officer. Five years later, she realized that to get a better job, she would need to acquire new skills and training in a different career path. She had always wanted to be a Project Manager, so she carried out general research and discovered that Google offered a six-month online Google Project Management program that came with a professional certificate. It was easy to enrol as it required no degree or experience. Under the space of six months, she learned in-demand skills that made her job-ready and now she works as an intern with a Project Management Consultancy. Today, Nina is well on her way to becoming a Project Manager.

Consider Your Values: Your values can also play a role in defining your career goals. What is important to you? Do you want to work for a company that is socially responsible? Do you value work-family-life balance?

Set SMART Goals:

Set goals that are Specific, Measurable, Achievable, Relevant, and Time-bound (**SMART**). For example, your goal might be to land a job as a marketing manager at a technology company within the next three years.

Story: Selfa had been working in sales for ten years, but he wasn't happy with his job. He felt like he wasn't making a difference in the world and wanted to pursue a career path that allowed him to give back. Selfa decided to explore career options that aligned with his values and discovered that he was passionate about environmental conservation. He researched how to begin his journey as an environmental conservationist. He set a **SMART** goal to land a job as a sustainability coordinator within the next two years. He began to read literature, take online courses and attend webinars online while participating in physical events where he could talk to people who were willing to point him in the right direction.

Conclusion:

Assessing your skills and defining your career goals is an important first step in finding your dream job. By identifying your strengths and interests, researching career options, and setting **SMART** goals, you can discover your true passions and find a job that is the right fit for you. In the next chapter, we will explore how to create a job search plan that will help you land your dream job.

— 2 —
PINPOINTING THE JOB

Crafting a Winning Job Search Strategy: Maximizing your search efforts for optimal results

Looking for a new job in any country with a sizeable population can be a daunting task, especially in today's competitive job market.

There is no one-size-fits-all approach to the job hunt. What may be a great strategy for one person may not be the best for another. With so many job seekers vying for a limited number of openings, job hunting can quickly become long-term and frustrating. It is important to have a realistic, but winning job search strategy in place to maximize your search efforts and increase your chances of success. Let's discuss some key components of starting on your journey looking for employment.

Identify Your Career Objectives and Strengths

In the previous chapter, we talked about assessing skills and defining career goals. This is a required initial step of self-introspection and examination to dig out all you know and all you do not know. This enables you to find out the skills you have and do not have, and how to go about equipping yourself with the requisite skills in order to find a career pathway suitable for you. This is a time to be honest with yourself about what sets you apart from other candidates and what you can bring to the table as an employee of a prospective organisation.

Now that you have the skills or experience required, you will need a work environment to practice what you've learned and become proficient at it. It's important as you journey, to have a clear understanding of your career goals and strengths. This will help you focus your search efforts and identify the right opportunities when they pop up.

1. Determine Your Career Objectives

Ask yourself a few questions. What type of job do I want? What kind of industry do I want to work in? What level of responsibility do I want? Be specific and realistic about what you want. Make sure you put down all your personal brain storming in writing, so that you do not miss out on anything or any ideas. That way you can go over what you have written to discover what is unnecessary and also find out which of your expectations are realistic. Your goals and desires should take into account your skills, experience or lack thereof, training and education. As you ascertain these, you are well on your way to hitting your personal developmental objectives and becoming what you want to be.

2. Join Online Professional Platforms

Once you've identified your career objectives, ensure you join online professional platforms like LinkedIn and other related online groups. These professional platforms are designed to provide relevant information about different work sectors and industries. They also post daily opportunities for job seekers. In addition, they provide free tutorials, professional tips and counsel on how to get into a particular career and what to do to excel in it.

2a. Using LinkedIn™ to Get Noticed By Recruiters & Employers

Many people share everything they know on LinkedIn for free. Recruiters, who are usually inundated with CVs and resumes, have since seen LinkedIn as a top recruiting tool for securing competent candidates. Most recruiters check out your LinkedIn and your general social media profiles. Edit your SM platforms to showcase your professional personality. It's the small adjustments we make that help greatly in this journey. Small improvements like an impressive headshot go a long way to make a great first impression.

In short, these platforms should be checked daily just like a Pastor checks his bible every day for guidance. And like the good book says in the latter part of Proverbs 3:5, when it comes to knowledge in general, "…do not lean on your own understanding." There are always people who know better than you and are open to helping you realize your professional dreams.

3. Use Dedicated Job Search Engines

Agreed, it is often difficult finding the right job for your professional development, but having the right mindset when starting off on your job search is key. Hopefully, there is no challenge that a positive and determined mindset from the onset cannot overcome. Thankfully, too, there are specialized job search tools like Jobberman, Indeed, and others that are useful for job searches. You can easily browse thousands of job postings from companies across the country using these search engines, which make it possible for you to find the appropriate employment for your qualifications and skills very quickly.

First set up an account with the respective job search engine(s) of your choice. Under this account, upload your CV/Resume. Make sure you have updated your CV to showcase your strengths and skills before uploading. After that, customize your page to receive job alert notifications. You may narrow your search using a variety of criteria including keywords such as job titles, locations, skills, and more on majority of these job search engines. This is a great technique to use to shortlist the number of available positions. It will help you to keep up with the most recent job openings, and from the job alerts you receive, you can start applying directly to the companies for positions that match your skillsets, strengths and educational qualifications. Job search engines are a great way to save time as they make it easy to upload your CV, cover letter, and other documentation related to the job application process.

Things to Consider When Looking at Job Vacancies on Job Search Engines

1) When researching on the various job-search tools out there, take note of the features that each platform offers, such as job notifications, résumé writing, career counsel, and job recommendations.

2) Register with job search engines that give you many options and flexibility to learn more about the position and application process. To find the kind of employment you're interested in, make a note of employers that you come across as well as job postings that are available.

3) Ensure that you retain a record of all the job advertisements you respond to. Make a note of the organization, the position title, the application date, and any comments you received. You can capture the page digitally and save it in your job folder.

4) Keep an eye out for fresh job listings on job search engines. When a new position matching your qualifications is listed, several job search engines offer job notifications that can send you an email.

4. Networking as a Successful Job Search Technique

One of the most effective resources for a job hunt is networking. It entails building connections with individuals in your field or industry who can help in your search for employment. The job hunt process is not complete without networking because networking can lead to new chances and offer insightful information about the job market.

While networking requires time and effort, it is worthwhile. It takes more than just relying on newspaper job postings and job advertisements online to conduct a fruitful job search. Reaching out to individuals in your profession and within your sector who can give you the

kind of information and resources you need to get the ideal job is another key requirement. Join professional associations or online discussion groups to stay up to date on industry trends and to connect with potential employers. Take the time to build relationships with people in your field and industry. They may be able to help you find the job you're looking for.

You can start by having a credible internet presence as it is one of the best methods to begin networking. Social media networking is a popular tool used by recruiters and businesses to locate potential recruits. As earlier mentioned, make sure you have a credible LinkedIn page and if necessary, register with other social media platforms. This will make a positive first impression on recruiters and possible employers, as well as help you network with other professionals in your field. It is important you connect with employers on social media. Many employers use social media as a way to recruit new candidates. Follow companies and industry leaders on social media and comment on their posts to get your name out there. You can also send a direct message to their inbox if their message icon is enabled.

Attend career fairs, industry events, conferences and seminars as this will afford you the opportunity to meet people in your field. Career fairs give you the opportunity to meet with the employers and human resource managers of organizations you may want to work with. These senior executives are usually friendly, approachable and ready to tell you strategies and ways to get employment in their organizations. In addition to networking with people in your field, you should also network with people outside your industry. You never know who may be able to provide you with valuable information or contacts that can help you in your job search.

Finally, be sure to tap into your personal network. Reach out to your friends, family and colleagues. Tell them that you are looking for a job. Ask them if they know of any opportunities or if they can tell any employers of labour that you are looking for a new job. Your friends, family, and acquaintances may know someone who's looking for someone with your skills and experience. Ask them to keep an eye out and pass along information if they hear of any job openings.

Networking opens up new opportunities and provides valuable insight into the job market. With a well-executed networking strategy, you can find the job you're want.

It's important to remain upbeat and confident during the job search process. Keep in mind that you possess attractive traits and skills that set you apart from other candidates and will get you noticed by the right employers and organizations sooner or later. Remain focused on your objectives and keep in mind that the job search process is a journey that can result in more favourable circumstances.

— 3 —

PUTTING YOURSELF OUT THERE

Distinctive CV/Resumes, and Job Application Cover Letters: Designing materials that capture attention

As the title suggests, the goal is to make documents like your CV, which is short for Curriculum Vitae, standout so that they can be noticed. For something to be distinctive, it has to be unique or intentionally different in such a way they literally pop. In other words, your information should be presented in a professional and visually appealing way.

What Does a CV, or Curriculum Vitae, Mean?

CV is the Latin expression "curriculum vitae," which approximately translates to "course of life." A CV is a written summary of a person's education, professional experience, accomplishments, and other pertinent credentials.

A CV is often used in academic, scientific, or research fields and is longer than a resume. It is also widely used in countries where employers expect to see a more detailed summary of a candidate's qualifications.

A well written CV should include sections on education, work experience, publications, presentations, research experience, academic honours and awards, professional affiliations, and other pertinent information. It is crucial to modify your CV for each job application, emphasizing the credentials and experiences that are most relevant.

What is a Resume?

Unlike a CV, which is often longer and more detailed, a resume is a document that provides a concise summary of a person's education, work experience, skills, and other relevant qualifications.

A resume is usually one to two pages in length and is tailored specifically to the job for which the person is applying. A well-written resume can help a job seeker stand out from other applicants and increase their chances of being invited for an interview.

A resume will include sections on education, work experience, skills, and other relevant information, such as volunteer work or professional affiliations. It may also include a summary or objective statement at the top of the page, highlighting the person's skills and qualifications and expressing their interest in the job.

It is important to tailor your resume for each job application, highlighting the skills and experiences that are most relevant to the position you are applying for. This can help you make a positive impression on the employer and increase your chances of being invited for an interview. Note however, that the terms CV and Resume as used here are often applied interchangeably except otherwise stated.

Writing a Distinctive CV/Resume

In some places, the terms CV and Resume are used

interchangeably. The explanations below can be applied to both in that sense.

1. **Research the Organization You are Applying to:** Before you can write a distinctive CV, you must first understand the nature of the job application that the CV is meant for. As a candidate, you must be sufficiently interested in the position to take the time to make your application stand out. If you go in with a generic CV for all positions, HR managers can tell that you did not spend time researching the company. You will end up looking unserious and that is not a first impression you want to create. Learn more about the organization you are applying to by checking out their website. Make sure you understand the company's goals, principles, products and services. Having this information will enable you to design your resume and cover letter with useful key words that are pertinent to securing the job. It will also appeal to the HR Manager and get your CV through to the selection stage.

2. **Highlight Significant Accomplishments and Skills:** If you meet over 60 – 70% of the primary requirements for a job, you can apply, but note that recruiters are reviewing hundreds of applications for various

positions. They screen those loads of CVs with a set of critical markers in mind, so make it simple for them to notice your CV and qualifications. I often advice candidates to apply the KISS principle when designing a CV. **KISS** is an abbreviation that stands for Keep It Simple and Short or Keep It Short and Sweet.

Emphasize the aspect of your abilities, training and

background that are most relevant to the position you are looking for. Include any honours, credentials, or other achievements that show the employer how qualified you are, and how valuable you will be to the organization.

3. Making Your CV ATS (Applicant Tracking System) Friendly

Use the proper format for your CV design. Preferably, make your CV ATS friendly. An ATS software is an Applicant Tracking System used by recruiters to track candidates and manage the recruiting and hiring process. Basically, an ATS software scans and stores CVs in a digital database from which recruiters shortlist applications by deploying certain keywords related to the position they want to fill. The reality is that recruiters receive over 150 and even up to a 1000 CVs for one advertised position. Imagine having to go through such massive volumes of CVs in order to fill one or two job positions. That is why up to 50% of recruiters use an ATS to help them shortlist the candidates who meet most of their critical requirements.

Now, the trick is to make sure your CV contains the relevant keyword pertaining to the position for which you are applying. Recruiters usually use keywords that contain specific skills, job titles, responsibilities, professional certifications or qualifications, etc. to seek out qualified candidates. The sensible place to start in order to know what keywords are relevant to a recruiter is usually by checking the vacancy e-flyer or advertisement post. This is why I always advice candidates not to use the lazy approach of sending in a generic CV for all job vacancies. Customise your CV to be purpose-specific. People who use a generic CV to apply for every job are unlikely to get picked. Customise your CV or cover letter to fit the job requirement each time. Insert precisely, the keywords indicated on the job post on your CV.

Remember that a CV is the tool you use to sell yourself as a viable product to an employer. That is where you describe yourself effectively. For instance, if the advert indicated "Head of School" as the position to be filled, and you have management experience running a school, make sure the word "Head of School" is listed on your CV along with the management experience you have acquired.

Design your CV/Resume with the following in mind:

- Mention the key skills relevant to the job you're applying for at the start of your resume. Your skills should always be right at the start of your resume, coming just after your name and profile summary.

- Itemise or breakdown your skill set to make it easier to identify the skill the hiring manager seeks in a candidate. Don't just say you have project management skills, mention the exact tools or app you are proficient at using like Gantt, WBS, etc. Don't just mention that you are digitally savvy, say you are good at graphic designs and knowledgeable in the use of Canva, familiar with the process of creating online survey tools or setting up zoom meetings, etc. Give specifics and not just general information.

- Use a formal style that is simple to read. The general rule of thumb is to use a white background with a plain text.

- Use no less than a 12-point font size, in black fonts like Times Roman or Garamond or Calibri. Don't apply anything fancy except you want your CV to showcase your talent as a lettering or script designer or some form of calligraphy expert related to the position you seek. Other than that, simple is the best.

- Use large job title headers and concise bullet points.
- Let your line spacing be 1.5 or 2.0 so that your words are not too clumped up.
- Remove borders, or coloured fonts, graphs and charts as some ATS software (Applicant Tracking System) do not accept it.
- Keep important contact information like your name, mobile number and email in the body of the CV document and not in the header or footer section unless it is required by the recruiter.
- Your CV should be aligned to the left with no less than half to one-inch margins.
- Submit your CV as a word document and not as a PDF document except it is so required.
- Note that CVs that are colourful with pictures and graphs may be pleasing to the eye, but not so pleasing to the ATS software which is automated

to be objective.

- Don't ever use coloured fonts to prepare your CV.

I had a candidate send me his CV in green font. It was distracting, unprofessional and outright irritating. Using coloured fonts on a CV is a definite no-no! A CV is a professional document that should be easy to read and understand. Using coloured fonts can make the document difficult to scan and interpret, and it can also make the applicant seem unserious or unprofessional. In addition, coloured fonts can be difficult to read on a screen or to print out. Overall, it's best to stick with a simple black font when writing a CV. It is much more professional and easier to read.

Example of Skills to Put in Your CV When Applying for a Specific Position

Example One - Data Analyst: Someone applying for the position of a Data Analyst should ensure they include the following in their CV and Cover letter:

1. Strong data analytical skills and experience.

2. Familiarity with data analysis tools such as SQL, Python, or R.

3. Ability to communicate complex data findings clearly and concisely.

4. **A link to your GitHub profile:** having a GitHub profile is a way to demonstrate a candidates coding expertise and experience. When it comes to a Data Analyst role, a GitHub profile can highlight your proficiency in handling data and code as well as your ability to collaborate with others on various projects. Additionally, it provides you with an opportunity to showcase any projects you have been involved in.

These four essential points would demonstrate a candidate's suitability for the role and highlight their skills and experience.

Example Two - Research Assistant: It is crucial that someone applying for the position of a Research Assistant include the following information in their CV and Cover letter:

1. Highlight any research experience you have such as projects you've been involved in or papers you've published.

2. Emphasize your skills in data analysis, interpretation and data visualization.

3. Demonstrate your ability to work both independently and collaboratively as part of a team.
4. Provide insights into your research methodology.

Explain how you gather, interpret and analyze data in order to draw conclusions from it. This will give prospective employers, hiring managers or recruiters, an understanding of your critical thinking abilities and capacity to work independently.

You see, Research assistants typically employ a range of methodologies and approaches to conduct their research, which vary based on the field and the specific project at hand. Some of the common methods they use include;

- Conducting surveys and interviews
- Engaging in observation and fieldwork
- Reviewing relevant literature and analyzing data
- Employing statistical analysis techniques
- Undertaking lab experiments
- Utilizing modeling and simulation approaches.
- Ethnography

These are just a few examples, but there are many other methods, techniques, skills that may be used. However, it is wise to demonstrate on your CV or Cover letter that you are familiar and competent with the use of these research techniques.

In summary, remember to tailor your application materials specifically to make a case for why you are the ideal candidate for that particular position you applied for.

> **Story:** Sadiq was quite knowledgeable in the use of Gantt charts to interpret data related to project management. A client wanted an Executive Assistant who was conversant with project management. In other words, what the client needed, after further clarifications in a needs assessment chat with the hiring manager, was an assistant who was knowledgeable about some of the project management tools. Sadiq sent in his CV which made no mention of Gantt or project management under its key skills. The client overlooked him, but during the interview, the hiring manager, identified that he was

excellent in the use of Gantt which was precisely what the client wanted. Sadiq almost missed the opportunity because he didn't highlight this in his resume. This is yet another reason not to send in a generic CV for all job vacancies. Your CV should be tailored to fit the position for which you are applying.

General Tip: Aim for a clean, uncluttered look that displays your experiences and skills on your resume without being unnecessarily complicated. Permit me to let you into a little secret: **the recruitment industry usually uses keywords and key terms to search out the right CVs.** These key terms could be a skill the client is in desperate need of like a working knowledge of Peachtree or Canva, or Gantt, or Education Marketer, or Content Creator, or Agile, etc. These are some of the key terms and phrases that might help employers/hiring managers find the CVs that are most relevant to their job openings.

4. Do Not Lie on Your CV: Do not put on your CV, anything that is false. You will be found out at least by people who do their jobs well.

My team interviewed a candidate for the position of a basic four teacher. Let's call him Jeff. The knowledge of French was not required for this position, but Jeff wrote on his CV that he could speak French.

He did well at the interview and was considered among the top 2 contenders for the position. At the end of the interview, one of the interviewers who noticed that he added French as one of the languages he could speak, asked him, *"Comment tu t'appelles?"*

Jeff was mute.

She asked another question in French, *"Comment ça va?"*

Once again, he remained unresponsive.
Finally, she asked,

"Parlez vous Francais?"

Jeff stared at everyone totally flummoxed.

He couldn't even respond with a *"Oui,"*

which showed he had no inkling of what she was saying. Yet, on his CV, he had included French as a language he could speak. He qualified for the job, but his lack of integrity led him to add on his CV that he could speak French beyond *bonjour*, which became his undoing. He didn't even need French for this position, so why put it on his CV? Now everyone on the panel stared at him as a liar and began to suspect everything he had said before. All because he reckoned he could embellish his CV with false details just to appear smarter. Although he aced the interview, he failed on values, and that was how his cookie crumbled. For those who buy into the Fake-It-Until-It's-Real ideology, do not try that on your CV.

Lying on your resume totally damages your credibility. Please be as authentic and sincere as you can. Although you may escape being discovered in the lies you told during the interview process, please remember that your sins will surely find you out. I'd rather employ a person with character and no skills and train him than one with skills and no character.

5. You Must Proofread: I cannot say this enough - the most important finishing touches to apply to any document, CV or cover letter is to proofread what you have written. Proofread, proofread, and proofread for typographical errors, silly mistakes, misspellings, grammatical errors, colloquial constructions, wrong jargons etc. In this era of social media, there is still nothing that gives a bad impression like a CV full of social media slangs or abbreviated words and inappropriate, informal language that make you appear like an unserious candidate.

6. Peer Review: Aside from checking your CV or cover letter for grammar and spelling mistakes, it is worth considering having it reviewed by a peer. Peer review involves asking someone, such as a friend or colleague, to read through your CV or cover letter and offer their feedback. This can be particularly beneficial if the reviewer has experience in the field you're applying to or is a writer. Peer review helps identify areas in your CV or Cover letter that may require improvement. The reviewer can give feedback on aspects like the structure, tone and clarity of your document.

Writing a Distinctive Cover Letter

What is a Cover Letter?
Basically, a cover letter is a document that accompanies

your resume or job application and gives the hiring manager, recruiter or prospective employer a brief introduction to your person. It is often a one-page document that outlines your qualities that are suitable for the job, including your skills, experiences, and education.

While your CV or Resume can get you through the door at the initial selection process, you can use your cover or application letter to further distinguish you from the rest of the candidates on a recruiter's shortlist. You see, a cover letter gives you the opportunity to sell yourself to the recruiter in a story format. Beyond objectivity, your cover letter makes you likable to the recruiter. A recruiter who likes your cover letter is more likely to select you from the rest of the candidates. The manner you communicate your enthusiasm, skills and passion stand you out. With your cover letter, you can explain away gaps in your CV that the recruiter might be concerned about. Your cover letter describes why your experience, skill sets and personality align with the position recruiters are seeking to fill. In short, if well written, this letter should be able to give a richer insight that communicates to the potential employer, all the other stuff about you that the CV does not usually portray like your personality, work ethos, values, your communication style, and your relatability skills.

What are some of the Essential Components that Recruiters look for in a Cover Letter?

As a recruiter, I would first look at your **Brief Introduction**. It explains who you are, mentions a specific advantage your experience or skill can bring to the table, and why you are interested in the job. It is advisable you do this in a one-page document that outlines your suitability for the job, and that typically highlight your abilities, experiences, and education. Mention relevant qualifications, experiences and skills that make you a good fit for the job. You should be able to convey excitement about working with the organisation and be somewhat knowledgeable about the service it renders as well as show how you can help further its goals.

Example:

Dear *(Hiring Manager)*,

I hope this email finds you well. My name is *(Name)*.

I am writing to express my interest in the position of *(position)* within your organization. management I have a background in accounting and project software. I believe that my unique blend of qualifications and experience would make me an excellent fit for the role.

I graduated from *(University)*, with a degree in *(field).* I have been actively working in *(the industry)* for *(the number of years.)* Throughout my career, I have gained expertise in (mention skills) and have successfully contributed to numerous projects in my line of work. Moreover, I am a highly motivated individual, undeterred by challenges and I thrive well as part of a team.

I am confident that my skill set and professional experience align perfectly with the requirements of this role. The opportunity to join your management consulting team excites me. I feel that my strengths lie in strategy development and planning which can significantly contribute to your organization's success.

Thank you for taking the time to consider my application.

I look forward to discussing how my qualifications align with your needs.

Best regards

(Name)

— 4 —

SELLING YOURSELF AT THE INTERVIEW

Nailing the Job Interview: Mastering the art of selling yourself at a job interview

As Job interviews can be a source of anxiety. It is usual to think that you are under scrutiny at every turn during the interview and worry that the answers you give will determine whether or not you get the job. And while that may be true to an extent, this kind of thinking creates unnecessary dread and worries. It is best to see job interviews as a positive opportunity to put your best foot forward, a time to showcase your qualities and sell yourself to your prospective employer. In reality, interviews are a chance for you to promote yourself and show potential employers what you're worth. Let us look at some ways and techniques to help you ace the job interview and perfect the art of selling yourself.

Tip 1: Do your Homework – First Research the Organization

First things first. It is crucial to prepare for your interview way before the appointment. Learn as much as you can about the company's history, goals, values, and ongoing projects before your interview. The interviewer(s) can tell if you checked the organisation's website and social media pages or not. Doing so provides you with information about the company that you can use when giving answers to some of the questions you will be asked at the interview. It shows that you are serious about the position and have gone above and beyond in your preparation in order to respond to queries effectively and display the attributes of the kind of knowledgeable and proactive candidate they want to occupy that position. It puts your interviewers at ease immediately.

Tip 2: Practice your Elevator Pitch or Speech Well Ahead of Time

An elevator pitch is a brief introduction of who you are to the interviewer. It is the answer to questions phrased in this manner: "Please tell us about yourself or kindly introduce yourself and tell us why you are here?" It is usually a short summary of who you are in no longer than 2 minutes and can be as short as 30 seconds. It is called an elevator pitch because it is meant to be delivered within the time span it takes for an elevator ride. In a nutshell, it should spell out who you are, what you do and what you hope to do at the organization if employed. **Keep it brief**. Start or end with your name. Mention the skills and qualifications you have that are specific to the job and end with the goals you want to achieve if you are given the opportunity to occupy the position for which you have applied. This is your chance to make a great first impression on the hiring manager.

If you are looking for a role in say, Digital Marketing, you are expected to mention that you are savvy with digital marketing tools and you can list a few of them like email management and automation, knowledge of the use of Mailchimp and administering survey questionnaires. You can say how you are great at creating SEO and attractive social media contents. You can also mention that you carried out a marketing campaign for an organization where you promoted their product to potential customers that resulted in conversions and increase in sales by say 30%. You could state the ecommerce sites you have worked on and the technological tools you used etc. Your pitch is a time to demonstrate how effective you are in performing your job, duties and responsibilities efficiently. Since you are meant to have this pitch covered under 2 minutes, it means you must put in the time you need to practice your speech either with a friend or in front of a mirror so as to cut out the parts that are irrelevant and perfect the essentials of your speech.

Smile: Start your pitch with a confident smile as it shows you are comfortable and know what you are doing, even if you feel nervous inside.

Say Your Name.

Do Not Speak Too Fast. Yes, we know you may have only 2 minutes, but speaking too quickly can throw you off, as it might cause you to ramble, send you into a panic, and make it difficult for your listeners to follow your sentences if they are all jumbled up.

Define Your Value Proposition: The distinct advantage you provide clients or employers is your value proposition. It should be focused on addressing a particular need or problem.

Practice Until You Can Say it in Your Sleep. A lot is riding on those first 2 minutes, so it is wise to practice and rehearse until you have nailed your speech to a T. Try it out in the shower, in front of your mirror, practice it with a friend, repeat it on walks, on the treadmill and everywhere you can, until you've honed it down to a perfect finish.

Guidelines on Creating Your Elevator Pitch. See some good examples below:

EXAMPLE A

My name is Ven Zitta. I am a Microsoft certified Website Developer with over 5 years of experience. I develop user-friendly, SMART website platforms within the space of 8 weeks and provide free website support for 12 weeks subsequently for my clients. I have developed over 20 websites. Some of my clients include, Zenith Bank, SLK Fitness Centre, KPMG, Vivian Martha High School, etc.

EXAMPLE B

My name is Peter Lar and I have been a chartered accountant for over a decade, working with different financial institutions in Lagos, Abuja and Plateau State. I help small and medium sized business owners save money on their taxes and increase profits. I provide tailored financial solutions for businesses and the financial insights you need to make smart business decisions. From bookkeeping to tax planning, I can help you achieve your financial goals and grow your business if given the opportunity to head your accounts department.

EXAMPLE C

I am a graduate of Mass Communication from the University of... As a student, I was part of volunteers who published and distributed the UJ Newsletter for the University's Media Unit, and later became the student head of Faculty News for the Faculty of Arts and Humanities on Campus. This position required that I write a weekly column in our school bulletin which I did successfully for the 12 months of my tenure as Head of News. Recently, I completed my NYSC programme with Channels Television Network. While serving at Channels Television, I worked as a reporter covering the segment called "Everyday Lives." I am good at writing compelling story lines about the challenges faced by ordinary people. This has equipped me with some practical reporting and content creation skills which I hope to put into good use if given the opportunity to be the Assistant Content Creator on your TV Soap series. I also have a strong letter of recommendation from the Head of Programmes for Channels Television here with me. I believe my strength in research and editing, storytelling, and media report writing will add to the success of your TV programmes. My name is Yewande Davis.

Tip 3: Dress Appropriately

Dressing well for an interview is incredibly important, as it creates a strong first impression and shows that you take the occasion seriously. For young professionals in the Tech industry, it's important to strike a balance between looking professional and personable, while also showing off your style and individuality. For men, a well-tailored suit, polished shoes, and a clean-cut look are always a good choice. For women, a professional dress or skirt/fitted trousers and blouse with simple jewelry and understated makeup can be appropriate. In either case, dressing well shows that you're prepared, confident, and professional.

Tip 4: Do Not Lie about Your Past or Actual Remuneration:

During the recruitment process, usually at an interview or afterwards, it is crucial that you are honest and transparent when providing information about your past or actual remuneration figures. Falsifying or misrepresenting such details can have serious consequences, including the risk of losing a new job opportunity. Recruiters, HR Officers or Employers often conduct thorough verification or reference checks to confirm the accuracy of the information provided. If any differences or contradictions are found during these processes, it could result in the job offer being revoked or withdrawn. These actions, not only put your reputation at risk but also erode trust with potential employers. It is essential to prioritize integrity and honesty when discussing payment and benefits making sure that your behaviour aligns with standards and professional values.

In Summary, when you are going for an interview, ensure you do this:

Be Ready for Your Next Interview!

An interview is your time to shine and impress. It is the test of all the hard work you've put in to get to that point where you are invited for a formal chat. You really don't want to mess that up do you? To be honest, interviews can be rattling even for the brave ones amongst us. So let me rephrase the question: do you get tense and overtly worried when you have an interview to attend? I do as well but these few helpful tips will get you prepared and make you feel more confident about your next interview.

Get an Interview Folder:
Why do you need an interview folder? It presents you as someone who is organized and professional. It helps you keep track of all the essential documents you may need to take to the interview venue. Interview folders come in all sizes. Just get one that serves your purpose, something that keeps your documents neat, unruffled and protects it from the rain or from getting stained or messed up.

Get Copies of Your CV/Resume Ready:
Yes I know, you already sent copies of your CV to the interviewer but another sensible thing you need to do is make some extra copies for your home file. Print it out from soft copy to hard copy. Ensure you put at least two to three copies in your interview folder.

Get Some Good Writing Stationaries.
Ensure you have up to three very good writing pens.

You don't want to have just one pen in case you lose it or loan it out to someone who didn't return it or worse, the only pen you have stops working just when you really need to jot something down. Have a notepad for taking notes. Avoid papers as they can easily get missing. But if you must use paper sheets then clip them together. Put all of these items in your interview folder and smaller items in the folder pockets alongside your business cards, if you have some. Some folders can take a mini-iPad or electronic pad.

Make Sure You Do Your Research about the Organization:

By showing that you are knowledgeable about the organization you hope to work for, you make the interviewer believe in you more than the others. Reading up about the organization helps you to tailor your responses to fit with the organizational goals of the company. You will be able to give more meaningful answers to the questions asked of you and it would also prepare you to ask intelligent and relevant questions in return.

Dress to Fit the Position You Want:

Your appearance at an interview gives the very first impression about you and you want that to be a good one. Look sharp and professional. Wear colors that are not riotous or inappropriate for the position. Let your attire be fitted and convey a sense of confidence, modesty and respectability.

Be Mentally Prepared:

Take Take time and think about the position you are being interviewed for and dwell a bit on the different expectations and responsibilities that it would demand from you. Go through the most important questions that you are likely to be asked in your mind. Write down your best responses in your own words. Review your cover letter and your CV so as to be reacquainted with the information you provided to the recruiter when you applied for the position. This exercise is to make sure you are accurately aligned in your mind with what you wrote on paper and what you hope to say during the interview conversation. This is the time to prepare yourself emotionally, intellectually, psychologically and physically for the forthcoming interview. Practice your smile, sitting position, and how or where you want your hands to be during the interview - generally how you want to look as regards composure. If a walk would help clear your head, go for it. Some people stand in front of their mirrors and talk freely to themselves whilst others carry-out a mock interview with a friend. Do only what you are comfortable with when preparing for an interview. Do not over-task yourself physically. This has more to do with the mind than with the body. This is your get-it-to-ge-ther moment. Be prepared.

Be at the Interview Venue on Time:

This is very important. I would suggest one hour or an hour thirty minutes ahead of time if you can. Getting to an interview venue on time relaxes and prepares you for any eventualities. Some interviews are in very big and large hotel grounds. You might get to the gate or building 30 minutes before hand and still walk some distance to locate the exact interview room. You do not want to get to the interviewer looking all sweaty, ruffled up and agitated. Your goal is to present a calm, poised and prepared appearance to your interviewer. In addition, you need some time to take in the environment of your interview. Some organizations display on their walls, the work culture and ethics of the organization which you can absorb while you're waiting, in time to give you an advantage with your responses during the interview process.

These are some of the ways you overcome pre-interview jitters. Now go out there and nail that job! Good luck.

— 5 —

PUTTING A PRICE TAG TO YOUR SKILLS

Nailing Negotiating Salary and Benefits: Getting what you're worth

One of the most important steps in the employment search process is negotiating your pay, perks and benefits attached to the position you seek. Typically, an employer will present you with a compensation and benefit package. Sometimes this is done during the final interview process when management is seriously considering you for the position, and then subsequently put in writing with a proposed salary on your offer letter. Many employers usually start with a standard package. Some will try to offer you less than what you are worth if they feel they can get away with it, or if they sense you are desperate for the job. Do not look at salary negotiation as you look at a product with a price-tag in the open market or on a supermarket shelf. Those products are tangible goods which usually come with a fixed price. Sometimes, you may get a discount on an item. You, on the other hand are not a tangible product. You are a human being with dynamic needs and if those needs are not met in the long run, it may affect your level of productivity. So how do you negotiate your salary in such a way that you are adequately compensated for your skills, character, experience and education?

Here are a few pointers to getting started on your salary negotiation:

First, find out what the average salary is for that role. This means, you should carry out your own research about the salary expectancies surrounding such roles. Do not be afraid to ask around. Check websites like payscale.com and glassdoor.com, then be realistic with your offer. If you are living in a large city, factor in which part of the city you may be coming from to get to your office. You should factor in the cost of your daily transportation if you're using public transport or cost of fuel if you are using your own private vehicle.  Some organizations provide a separate transport or accommodation allowance in addition to your net salary payment. Some have a benefit package that comes with pension and a National Health Insurance Scheme. Others, go the whole nine yards and provide official transport, accommodation, health insurance, holiday perks, etc.

Always start salary negotiations on a positive but honest note. Show enthusiasm about your eagerness to add value to the organization that goes beyond merely receiving a monthly pay out. In addition, be clear about the job descriptions and role expectations in discussions with your prospective employer. I cannot emphasize this enough. Please make sure you clarify your responsibilities. Clarify tricky phrases like "Property Clause," often used to cover business, ideas and products generated under the company as being owned by the company. Ask if the term "Property Clause" refers exclusively to properties generated for the company in the course of executing its operations. Ask for explanations for any other ambiguous terms in your offer letter. You will need to know in order to avoid future conflicts of interest or worse still, a lawsuit. Ensure the daily work hours is defined. If the salary does not seem to align with your realistic salary projections and does not factor in your years of experience, skills, education, and other value you know you will be bringing to the table, then boldly negotiate for more money. In the event you cannot get more money like in the case of a Candidate, Dino, who was offered a job he earnestly needed, he negotiated that the work tools provided for the job which included a laptop and an internet modem be his to claim a year from his date of employment offer, plus a thirteenth salary payment for the festive month of December.

In other words, you can suggest other forms of compensation that are beyond cash or financial emoluments. Some candidates ask for stock or equity options in the company, and ensure it is given in written form. Some ask for their names to be put on a product or to be given credit for a product design.

You should have this in mind when negotiating salary:

Be Clear, Be Confident: clarity means you know precisely your worth which is defined by what value you are bringing to the table. Mention your unique skills and the valuable experience you will bring in carrying out your duties. This will help you justify why you are asking for a particular figure. Tell them you have every confidence that they will offer you an appropriate wage that is both motivating and demonstrative of your worth and abilities. By so doing, you are also demonstrating your trust in their judgment and their ability to be fair.

Listen to the Offer Speech of the Employer/Hiring Manager. Pay close attention to what they say to you during the final stages when an offer or negotiation is on the table. Be attentive to what the employer is saying as you can pick out underlying messages or ideas from what is said or left unsaid. The employer could inadvertently but casually say that the organization is moving to a permanent location in a few months' time with free but limited accommodation for staff. You might then ask to be given free accommodation as part of your package. Or there could be mention of limited three-month training slots available for senior or middle management staff which you could easily get in on during negotiations.

> **Story:** Laura had always wanted to do her CIPD but didn't have the time or money for it. During the offer/negotiation discussions, the CEO mentioned that the company would be sending 3 staff for CIPD training under the Staff Development and Training Policy and she jumped on it. They were not willing to pay for vacations nor to give her a salary increase after 6 months, but were willing to pay for the CIPD training she desperately needed. This was because staff training ranked high in the work culture of this organization. It was a Win-Win situation at the end of the day. In recruitment, we call this kind of Win, non-salary benefits under professional development.

Be prepared to walk away from an unattractive offer. If, at the end of the day, your negotiations did not amount to any worthwhile trade-offs and produced nothing attractive or favourable to you, be prepared to walk away from the job offer. Sometimes the rigidity of an employer during negotiations is a sure sign of a difficult workplace or an awful boss. If you are desperate to hang on to a job, your desperation will show and that makes it even more difficult to get what you truly deserve.

Your body language during negotiations says a lot about you. Make sure you appear calm and not impatient. Do not let them hurry you into accepting an offer on the premise of a future review that is only verbally implied. Employers are not beholden to any promises that are not put into writing as that is not a binding contract. Some employers are known to feign amnesia or ignorance over verbally made promises which were never put in written form and which can therefore be easily denied.

— 6 —

GIVING VALUE WHEN YOU GET ON BOARD

*Excelling iin Your New Role at the Work Place:
Strategies for long-term success*

You've finally landed that new position you worked so hard to get. It doesn't matter if it is a promotion at your place of work or a new job at a new organization, congratulations to you! You deserve it. You earned it. Your excellence, your efforts, or even sheer grace may have given you this opportunity. It is one you are feeling quite ecstatic about and rightly so. Now, you don't want to mess this up, neither do you want to fail. Getting here has not been easy, and if you are wise, you want to make a huge success out of things, give the right impression to your bosses, and give your colleagues little to complain about.

Ensure You Understand Your Employer's Expectations

The question to ask yourself here is: what will make me more impactful to my employers in this role I occupy? In today's competitive career landscape, employers are looking for staff who are proactive and who have initiative; staff who are ready to disrupt the status-quo by injecting fresh ideas at work with a view to churning out better results.

This is the time to talk to your supervisor or boss. Ask them what kind of results they would like to see that will please them. Agreed, you have a general idea of what they want you to do, but now you want the specifics of what it is that you must do on this job that would make them satisfied with your output. Define these clearly into Quality Deliverables or Competence Categories in your own terms or words. I choose to use these 3 terms:

High-Quality Deliverables: Here you'll have high competence work duties.

Medium-Quality Deliverables: Have medium competence activities and

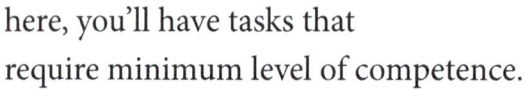

Low-Quality Deliverables: here, you'll have tasks that require minimum level of competence.

Your deliverables are usually stuff you are meant to achieve by a set deadline. They could be result-oriented or behaviour oriented. They could be daily, weekly, monthly or yearly and they add up to earn you the description of a competent and dependable worker. You want to be appraised as a competent staff and we know that competency grows with training, repeated practice, consistency, and experience.

High-Quality Deliverables: Be your own Assessment Evaluator. Usually, you should start by looking through your job description and key responsibilities. Break your tasks and responsibilities into daily, weekly, monthly and quarterly deliverables, then further into short term, medium term, and long-term goals if you can. Duties under this category may include:

Ensuring you understand the Company's Work Culture. Get to know your colleagues and team mates. Also look at what your coworkers are doing to get an idea of how good or how bad they are at performing their duties. You don't want to underestimate their abilities or overestimate yours. Be friendly and personable with people at your office, it paves the way for a more peaceful, cooperative and interactive working environment. We don't want you making enemies on your first day at work, do we? Not at all. Although sometimes, just being the newbie sets you up for resentment or the fireworks of office politics. Be on the alert for tricks and traps from office people who resent your presence and be on the alert too to receive good tips from people who mean well for you. Seek out opportunities to collaborate with colleagues where possible, as it fosters an atmosphere of excellent team synergy.

Duties under this category may include:
- Developing and implementing new products or services like a new app
- Carrying out complex financial analysis

- High-level contract and agreement negotiations
- Creating a fresh strategy for the organization
- Developing a new training curriculum
- Securing business from a top tier management consulting firm
- Conducting strategic training and presentations for senior level management

Medium-Quality Deliverables: In order to be a high achiever, you are better motivated when you put the expectations of your employer in the category of your medium quality deliverables so that you can push yourself to exceed their expectations. Since you are aiming for your own high-quality deliverables, your efforts will always be geared toward delivering results that exceed your medium goals. This is your own appraisal standard for gauging your work place performance. Your aim really, is to set a standard that keeps you above expectations or at the very worst, at the exact point of your employer's optimal performance which is your own Medium-Quality Deliverable point. Of course, we don't want to ever see you in the Low-Quality vicinity which your performance monitors must earmark as the Red-Alert Signal zone.

Duties under this category may include:
- Creating or drafting contents to post on the company's social media page daily or weekly
- Conducting market research and analysis
- Creating and implementing marketing campaigns
- Providing technical advice, support, or expertise to clients
- Carrying out routine financial analysis
- Developing and implementing strategies for operations
- Coordinating and supervising the work of your juniors, assistants or subordinates

Low-Quality Deliverables: activities carried out here may be the usual mundane/routine office stuff. It may be simple administrative tasks like updating customer data daily, but when this routine work is left undone for 2 weeks, it piles up and becomes a bulky and tedious work load that will still have to be tackled eventually. Not getting it done may end up making you look disorganized and once you appear messy to your supervisor, it will reflect on your appraisal sheets as "has a high tendency to procrastinate routine office duties." You don't want that.

Duties under this category may include:
- Posting of content already drafted on the company's social media page at a set time, say everyday by 2 pm
- Performing routine administrative tasks
- Data entry and filing
- Answering calls and responding to emails
- Handling and operating basic office equipment
- Maintaining, cleaning and rearranging work spaces, etc.
- Restocking office supplies

Story: Mark worked with Media Viva Event Company who regularly covered celebrity events around the city. The team responsible for shooting videos out on the field would usually send Mark, who was stationed at the office, a 30 to 60-second clip which he would upload immediately on the company's website for the viewing pleasure of followers of the event and the visitors who thronged their website for celebrity news. On this occasion, he needed to finish a pending status report which was one of his medium quality deliverables. When the video clip came in, he reckoned that he was too busy to post it immediately as his report was due in 2 hours. He would post it after he had sent in his report. He forgot. The next day, he was again engrossed in another important task, and decided that he would post the delayed videos which had now become 2 pending videos later in the day. Once again, he became engaged in other more pressing tasks, and soon, 2 videos became 3, and then 7 pending videos.

Mark knew he couldn't delay posting the videos any longer. He came to the office early the next day to upload all the videos at once. To his dismay, the internet server was down as there had been a storm the night before. The Public Relations Director of the company was soon tagged to a tweet from Viva fans complaining that the usual 60-second Celebrity Event Coverage clips which fans enjoyed on Viva Media's Website weren't forthcoming as they used to be. The director thought that rather strange, quickly checked the Viva website, and found their complaints to be true. Guess who got a strongly worded reprimand for embarrassing the company on social media?

You got that right, Mark! That query, over duties he tagged low-quality deliverables, cost him his promotion and other travel benefits that year.

Lesson: a drop in performing your low-quality deliverables can lead to high-cost outcomes!

Once you have understood your key performance indicators (KPIs), they become your work place productivity index. You can now go right ahead and exceed management's expectations. Functioning at your new role with this level of competence leaves a lasting impression on your subordinates, your colleagues, your supervisors and ultimately, your employer.

— 7 —

MOVING FORWARD ON YOUR CAREER PATH

Navigating Career Transitions: Pivoting with purpose

The process of making significant changes to one's professional path is known as a career transition. It often entails acquiring new skill sets, changing industries and having new responsibilities.

It is no surprise that more and more people are making career changes in their lives. Jobs that weren't available ten years ago, have appeared on the labour market. New technologies and innovations have sprung up. Hitherto, people were unfamiliar with work terms like Solar Engineer, Social Media Manager, Digital Marketer, Cyber Security Manager, and even terms that define workspaces like Remote or Hybrid employment. The advent of internet and all the successive technological innovations and changes that followed, disrupted the traditional kind of occupations and professions and changed the nature of the work environment. New skill sets had to be developed and learned. Online classes via different platforms like YouTube, webinars, etc. became feasible and necessary for many who needed tutoring online. Gradually, people became aware that better salary compensations were offered to digitally savvy employees. Most traditional office employees who lacked digital skills found themselves at the receiving end of the short stick in the labour market as they were easily replaceable or their skill sets were no longer needed or sought after unlike before.

The whole world has undergone drastic change. The COVID pandemic became one of the catalysts that quickened that change to our doorsteps. And now, we find ourselves reevaluating our career choices. The values we thought we brought to the work place have been replaced by other needs and values. Employers are seeking software developers or people with technical knowledge of certain software applications or hardware. These new occupations come with novel challenges. Top tier Management Consultants find themselves in need of new and quick problem solvers at an increasing rate. It is no wonder many are facing difficulties and getting frustrated working at jobs they thought they would outlive. For some, fear of the unknown and the uncertainties of the ever-changing imperatives of the labour market have crippled their lives and stopped them from taking proactive action. Every waking moment is filled with dread of the future.

If you are looking to switch roles or change careers, I want to assure you that this fearful trembling need not be the case with you. We know that fear incapacitates people from thinking right, so first things first, kick fear out from your mind. Having the right mindset is very important when making crucial decisions like a career change.

Here are some steps to take when making a career transition:

Introspection: Sit down with yourself and do your own self-examination about what matters most to you at this point in your life. Identify what are your goals in life. List your core values, skills and principles and rank them according to their level of importance. If family is your number one priority, rank it as number one. If money or a high salary is your number one priority, rank it accordingly. What about job satisfaction, autonomy, independence, status, work load, work hours etc.? Do you want a job that allows you to get recreational vacations? Or you want a job that leaves your weekends free? Under values, list those values that are important to you. Under skills, list the skills you have.

Changing Careers: If you are considering pursuing new career paths that appeal to your interests, you should start by making a list of the skills you have that are relevant to that role and career path. Also list the skills you do not have that are equally relevant to securing the role or career you want to pursue. There may be complementary skills you may need to acquire within your current pursuit for a higher position in your career or that will support your experience or extant skill sets; or you may need to do a total U-turn, a 360° turn around, where you may have to acquire new knowledge and training completely different from what you use in your present career.

If you are a secondary school teacher or an accountant or doctor who wants to be a lawyer then your journey will require that you factor in years of enrolment into a university to get a Law degree and be called to the Bar. This can take you close to 5 or more years to attain, depending on your country's education system. But that should not stop you if you are determined.

Become the Job

The world is developing rapidly.
If you look around you, you will find areas that are lacking skilled people to occupy them. You can decide

to venture into one such area through apprenticeship or enrolment in a skilled vocational acquisition program to get the knowledge and training you need to provide cutting edge solutions.

I have seen graduates learn carpentry after school so they could become furniture makers. I heard of a man who was concerned about the heaps of waste in his community. He enrolled for a waste management class and came back to his place to turn that waste into wealth. You can decide to pursue your interests which can lead to entrepreneurial endeavours, and end up developing a business model that can change your community. Case in point is the inspirational William Kamkwamba of Malawi, a young school boy, who hailed from a family of farmers. He was talented at fixing radios and other electronic gadgets for his friends, using materials sourced from the local junkyard. Faced with a family farm that had died because of lack of irrigation and access to water during the dry season, he developed a model windmill and later, a larger wind turbine, which he used to draw water from the village well and thus kept his family's farm irrigated. That was innovative and visionary of him. William ended up pursuing his engineering interests in environmental studies, built a solar powered water pump that supplied clean water in his village, and now works with Moving Windmills Project to build an Innovative Centre in Malawi where young people can create simple solutions to daily agricultural challenges.

Another example is the Nigerian inventor, Nnaemeka C. Ikegwuonu, who developed a solar powered refrigerator for farmers and villagers because they had no electricity in their community for use in preserving their fish, fruits and vegetable produce. He went on to install more than 30 Coldhubs and has saved over 20,000 tons of food from decay.

We have Elon Musk, a modern-day Da Vinci, whose creative inventions are redefining the world as we know it. From Tesla's revolutionary electric vehicles to SpaceX's trailblazing space technology, Musk's entrepreneurial genius has sparked a new era of innovation. Through his vision and ambition, Musk has carved out a niche for himself as one of the most influential figures of our time. His passion and drive are an inspiration to all who seek to create a better world. We are truly living in the age of Elon Musk.

You too can explore ways you can reinvent or develop new solutions to some of the pressing needs in your community. Most of today's innovations began with the desire to help solve communal or organisational problems. Focus is shifting away from college degrees to short vocational courses and industry certification. Vocational education now plays a critical role in preparing students, graduates and anyone who is willing to acquire new skills and meet the current realities of changing demands of employers and the labour market.

You May Not Be a Digital Native, but You Can Be a Digital Literate

It goes without saying that in the competitive job market of today, having in-demand skills is essential to getting hired. It's more crucial than ever to keep up with recent technologies and abilities due to the constantly changing nature of the workplace.

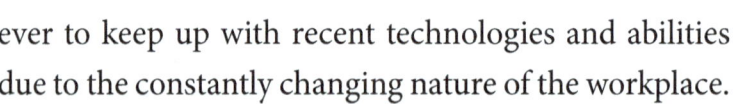

You will not only boost your earning potential and maintain your competitiveness in the work market, but it will also lead to new prospects. So, which talents should be prioritised?

I can tell you this for free because I am a recruiter: Digital literacy and technological proficiency, in my opinion, are crucial for success in the modern job market. You can build whatever interest or passion or career path you desire on the foundation of digital literacy because the world has gone digital. The birth of the computer, produced good fruits like smart mobile devices and gadgets, internet, software applications, and all sorts of online productivity tools that have brought the world right to you, to the tips of your fingers, a mere click away. The online community is dynamic and has flung wide the doors to every conceivable opportunity that access to a phone and/or internet can give. Use it!

Some of the likely questions to ask on your journey to a successful career path or business include:

What do I need to do to leave my current place for a better pay package?

How can I use technology to drive what I used to do

from an analogue to a digital model?

How can I communicate my ideas into a business model that is marketable?

How can I make my business scalable?

How can I get an internship or training opportunity?

Conclusion:

We live in a fast paced, rapidly changing orbit. Focus will always be on skills development and technical education in order to prepare human capital to acquire the skills for the ever-changing dynamics that the world of ICT, digitalisation and other innovative inventions have churned out. One must therefore have skills in order to belong in the 21st century global work force. The need to constantly update and enhance one's skills to keep up with the rapid pace of technological advancements is important. The world will continue to move forward with innovations which means there will always be the introduction of emergent technologies, tools, and processes. Therefore, individuals need to prioritize skill development to remain relevant and competitive in their respective fields.

Success in today's dynamic workplace requires lifelong learning and professional development. People can increase their marketability and ability to adapt to the changing demands of the global economy by keeping up with the most recent trends in their field. Additionally, keeping abreast of the latest advancements enables people to spot new opportunities and quickly adjust to market changes. In today's dynamic global market, lifelong learning is, in essence, a prerequisite for professional success.

So, get busy with learning and improving yourself. Let's get this employment/career vehicle out of the rut and unto the road. It's time to shift gears and learn to drive a new way.

You can reach the Author directly on her Social Media handles:
Facebook: Princess Chalya Miri-Gazhi
Instagram: @princesschalya
Twitter (X): @signetseal
TikTok: @signetseal (Princess Chalya)

www.ingramcontent.com/pod-product-compliance
Lightning Source LLC
Chambersburg PA
CBHW052101110526
44591CB00013B/2302